BRITISH FREIGHT TRAINS

John Jackson

First published 2017

Amberley Publishing
The Hill, Stroud
Gloucestershire, GL5 4EP

www.amberley-books.com

Copyright © John Jackson, 2017

The right of John Jackson to be identified as
the Author of this work has been asserted in
accordance with the Copyrights, Designs and
Patents Act 1988.

ISBN 978 1 4456 7268 7 (print)
ISBN 978 1 4456 7269 4 (ebook)

British Library Cataloguing in Publication Data.
A catalogue record for this book is available from
the British Library.

Typesetting by Amberley Publishing.
Printed in the UK.

Introduction

My earliest childhood memories include watching steam engines on the West Coast Main Line, particular on the section in Northamptonshire. Following steam's demise, diesel power, followed by electrification, became the order of the day as I grew up.

Since those days, the rail scene has changed dramatically. The railways are, of course, now privatised. Additionally, and for a number of reasons, many types of goods are no longer conveyed by rail. How many of us could have imagined a few years ago just how few coal trains would be running today. It should not be forgotten that over 11,000 merry-go-round coal hoppers were in use at the height of coal operations. This is not a historic review, however, nor or a debate as to whether or not privatisation was a good or bad move for the freight market.

Network Rail's latest advertising campaign claims that the railways today are carrying twice as many passengers as those of twenty years ago. I have no reason to refute that claim but ask any enthusiast and they will tell you of the downturn in non passenger traffic at their favourite location.

The unloved freight sector has few friends among the passenger train operating companies. After all, these companies stand accountable for their performance on punctuality and reliability within a railway that operates in a modern culture of blame. I've lost count of the number of times I've heard on-board announcements along the lines of 'We apologise for the delay. This is caused by us following a slow-running freight train' – or worse, 'because of a broken down freight train'.

Often freight and passenger operators share the infrastructure and sometimes this is detrimental to both. The importance of rail freight from Felixstowe, for example, is mentioned frequently in this publication. The Suffolk port may be among the UK's most important for handling container traffic but it is served by a short non-electrified branch line from Ipswich. Worse, this branch line has single track sections and shares this infrastructure with the class 153 unit operating a local passenger service.

So, let's take a quick look at the state of play for rail freight today. It is a railway that sees five main freight operators, namely: Colas Rail; DB Cargo (DB); Direct Rail Services (DRS); Freightliner (FL); and GB RailFreight (GBRf). These five main brands are all in competition for a piece of this freight action. This often results in customers moving their business from one operator to another.

Many examples of these past and present operations can be found in this book. Smaller freight operators such as Mendip Rail and Devon & Cornwall Railways are also included. All operators, large or small, are competing in a shrinking railfreight market. It is a market that has seen several changes of ownership of these brands in the years since rail privatisation.

The main operators also play an important part in helping continuously maintain and develop the rail infrastructure alongside internal 'customer', Network Rail. Their locomotives can be seen working on engineering duties for projects both large and small including track renewals, ballast drops and spoil removals. They play an important role in the autumn 'leaf fall' season with operation of Rail Head Treatment Trains (RHTT).

The types of locomotives used by these operators has also changed considerably in recent years. Some twenty years ago, Ed Burkhardt's Wisconsin Central Transportation Corporation purchased a number of the UK's newly privatised freight companies. With that acquisition came a pool of 1,500 or so locomotives. These locos were part of an ageing national fleet with an average age of around thirty years. The new business was soon to be renamed and branded as 'English, Welsh & Scottish Railway' – EWS.

These structural changes led to a defining moment in the recent history of railfreight traction in the UK. Almost immediately, EWS placed an order for 250 Class 66 locos to be built by General Motors at their London, Ontario (Canada) plant. The Class 66s were modelled in part on the successful Class 59 locos that had already been working in the UK (with what was to become Mendip Rail) for over a decade. EWS evolved over time to become Deutsche Bahn owned DB Cargo today.

The introduction of these Class 66 locomotives by EWS back in 1998 led to their becoming the most widespread loco type in use today. They are used by all five of our main UK operators.

Three members of the class have been withdrawn, namely DB 66048 (derailment at Carrbridge), FL 66521 (accident at Great Heck) and GBRf 66734 (Loch Treig derailment). Others have been stored out of use for many months now. Further, both DB and Freightliner have sent examples to work abroad in France and Poland.

By contrast, GBRf solved its locomotive shortage by purchasing several locos from owners in Holland and Germany. They were renumbered to 66747–66751. Further, they ordered new-build locos (to become 66752 onwards) from EMD in Indiana, USA. By then, the plant in London, Ontario, had closed. Despite this, almost 400 examples of the class remain on the UK operators' books today, accounting for the majority of freight traction movements in 2017.

Aside from the Class 66s, some variety of traction still exists. Survivors of both Class 37 diesel locos and Class 86 electrics see regular service despite having already celebrated their half centuries! The majority of the 100 Class 60s that date back to the end of the 1980s have been out of use for a number of years. In 2014, Colas purchased ten of these machines from DB Cargo. Of the ninety that remain in DB's hands, only a dozen or so currently see regular use. The majority of these remain languishing around DB's Toton depot area.

At the other extreme, recent builds of Class 68 and 70 diesel locos complement the freight traction base, with a number of other smaller class pools of various ages in between. We have even seen examples of Class 50 and 55 in revenue-earning service from time to time. Entertaining these distractions may be, but they don't materially affect the traction of choice today.

These loco types collectively bring the total loco fleet that can be considered as available for active service to around 600.

In addition to this large pool of locos a small fleet of four-coach Class 325 electric multiple units were ordered in the mid-1990s for limited Royal Mail work. A few sets see regular use notably between the rail/mail hubs in London, Warrington and Glasgow.

On the new loco delivery front, the beginning of March 2017 saw the first Class 88 DRS shipment reach Workington Docks with five classmates to join sister loco 88002 at Carlisle.

Colas's first loco of a new Class 70 order, 70812, also arrived in Liverpool Docks in early March 2017. This was the first of a batch of seven to extend their fleet and it was quickly put to use in the west of England.

The rail map has also changed considerably over the last twenty years. Gone are most station sidings and goods yards.

The rapid decline in the coal sector has seen most lines serving our collieries taken out of use. The ubiquitous Class 08/09 shunting locos are also fast becoming part of history.

Where yards still exist, there is a reduced need to shunt wagons and split trains as in the past. DB Cargo Class 60s and 66s are being used as yard shunters across the UK where needed. More often than not, that need is to support wagon movements for the Network Rail infrastructure market.

Instead, today's railway focuses on whole train movements over medium to long distance journeys. Freightliner themselves consider about 150 miles to be the shortest distance for rail to offer a viable transport alternative. Inevitably, a number of freight hotspots remain, while large parts of the rail network see little or no regular freight activity at all.

So, what freight traffic can be found on our rail network today? The most important are:

Goods in containers (particularly from the ports of Felixstowe & Southampton) and often described as intermodal/liner traffic.

Aggregates and other materials for the construction sector.

Oil and chemicals.

Coal and biomass.

Steel including ore and scrap metal.

Rail infrastructure maintenance and development.

These key markets are supplemented by a number of smaller sectors as diverse as cars, timber, domestic waste and nuclear fuel rods.

The freight companies have also found customers among the Passenger Train Operating Companies. Ross Taylor's excellent book *Main Line Locomotive-hauled Passenger Trains* covers this subject in detail. For this reason, this topic is only touched on here. As well as hauling passenger trains, the freight operators are often called on to haul empty passenger stock both on delivery as new – or for repair or overhaul to and from works. The Rail Operations Group (ROG) has joined the bigger operators in finding success in this market using a small fleet of handed-down locos.

No account would be complete without mention of the Channel Tunnel. Seen by many as a white elephant in terms of freight, its traffic volumes have never seemed to match its potential (at least to the rail enthusiast). The latest service to be inaugurated comes in the form of a service from China to Barking in Essex. This 'East Wind' service operated for the first time in January 2017, crossing ten countries and taking seventeen days on its 7,400-mile journey from China's Yiwu City before arriving in Barking. Locos 92015 and 66136 were given promotional branding for this inauguration.

British Freight Trains sets out to capture the variety of traction used in freight haulage in the last few years. Given the domination of the Class 66 in the sector, I hope shed lovers will forgive me for featuring a slightly higher proportion of the other classes in traffic in order to bring variety to the pages that follow; at least, it highlights the diversity of colour schemes and one-off liveries in use today. It's a far cry from the memories I have of the BR blue days when just the one colour/livery prevailed.

Finally, I often hear the question, 'where is the best place in the country for seeing freight trains today?' It's almost impossible to say, so no answers on that one here. I have my own favourites as these pages demonstrate. Sadly, the busiest for freight are not always the best places for photography. One such example is the Willesden area. Yes, freight traffic numbers are as high here as anywhere, but there are drawbacks. Most of the lines are wired. The WCML and the North London Line cross here on split levels. Additionally, some traffic bypasses the overbridge here completely by use of Acton Canal Wharf Junction or the Kensal Green chord.

In this book I have tried to offer a selection of locations as well as a mix of traction types. Whatever your personal preference for traction type, operator, or location, I hope you enjoy your journey!

The first numbered Class 66 was 66001. It was delivered in 1998 and is now in DB Cargo's revised red livery. It is seen here heading north through Sandy on 5 September 2016 working Plasmor empties from Bow to Heck.

The last Class 66 delivery included 66779. It was new to GBRf in February 2016 and carries the name *Evening Star*. Here it heads north through Doncaster on 5 July 2016 with empty sand hoppers from Middleton Towers to Monk Bretton.

Class 08 shunters are fast disappearing from the freight operators' books. Here, 08782 *Castleton Works* is on shunting duties in Doncaster's Up Decoy yard on 23 March 2015.

Another example, 08904, carries faded EWS livery. It shunts a Railvac in Eastleigh yard on 3 October 2015.

DB Cargo replaced many Class 08 duties with Class 60s and, more recently, Class 66s. Here 66082 is on yard shunter duties at Bescot on 18 March 2016.

Another 66 is captured on shunting duties on 5 October 2015. This time it's Freightliner example 66556 shuffling the fuel tanks on Ipswich stabling point.

Many DB Cargo locos have seen no use for many years. This is the view from Toton bank on 27 January 2017, it's a scene that seems timeless. 60067 leads a lineup of Class 60 locos that have been long stored.

By contrast, GBRf received its latest batch of Class 66s in 2016. On 15 February that year, 66708 *Jayne* makes a brief stop in Worcester Yard with new classmates (in order) 66777, 66776, 66779 *Evening Star*, 66778, 66774, 66773, and 66775. At the time 66779 was still tantalisingly under wraps, preventing the viewer from seeing its unique colour scheme.

Back in 2013, 66749 was another newbie for GBRf. It is seen on 26 June that year at Hillam Gates (Monk Fryston). It was on its way from Derby to Tyne Dock to commence its duties.

Another celebrity acquired by GBRF was 59003 *Yeoman Highlander*. It returned to UK from Germany via Immingham docks. It is seen here being dragged through Derby by 20311 and 20314 on 13 October 2014. Although it was to receive GBRf corporate colours, it retained its former Foster Yeoman nameplate.

The Tilcon traffic from Rylstone, near Skipton to Dairycoates (Hull) is one of the few regular freight workings through Leeds station. On 23 June 2015, 66232 is seen on the return working.

Soon afterwards, this working was to change operator from DB Cargo to GBRf. On 9 March 2016 that company's traction was 66764. It is again seen approaching Leeds station on the return westbound working.

Another working to change hands was the iron ore flow from Immingham to Santon (near Scunthorpe). On 15 November 2013, DB Cargo 60063 heads the westbound working through Barnetby.

In June 2016, Freightliner took over this operation in a deal with the then recently relaunched British Steel. Their traction on 2 February 2017 was 66605. It is seen approaching Barnetby station on the return working from Scunthorpe to Immingham Docks.

Direct Rail Services has been providing transport services to its parent company, Nuclear Decommissioning Authority, for over twenty years. On 11 June 2013, 20304 and 20302 head through Carlisle with a return working from Hunterston to their base at Sellafield.

A few days later, on 17 June 2013, the same pair of Class 20s – 20304 and 20302 – are seen working with 37423 *Spirit of the Lakes*. The trio are seen approaching the Tyne & Wear station at Pelaw on the return working from Seaham to Sellafield.

Another long-standing flow for DRS is the traffic emanating from Hinkley Point in Somerset. The first leg of the journey is from Bridgwater to Crewe. On 8 June 2016, 37605 and 37612 are seen heading north through Stafford heading for Crewe. The flasks will then be conveyed onwards to DRS's hub at Sellafield.

Over the years DRS has diversified into providing rail transport services to companies external to the nuclear industry. These duties include working with Network Rail over many years hauling a variety of test trains. On this occasion 37402 is used to haul *Caroline*, a rail inspection saloon. The photo is taken on 4 September 2014 as they approach Bedford.

Regular freight traffic in the south-west of England is sparse to say the least. The china clay industry remains the railway's chief customer in Cornwall. Traffic is centred on Goonbarrow (on the Newquay branch) and it is from here that the product is moved by rail to Fowey Docks for export. On 2 June 2016, out-based 66027 approaches St Blazey with a loaded working from Goonbarrow to Fowey.

The wagons from the above working lay over in St Blazey yard for several hours. This enables loco 66027 to work from St Blazey to Parkandillack. Both these workings head eastwards to run round in the loop at Lostwithiel. Barring problems, the loco for these diagrams spends several months out-based at St Blazey.

One of Colas Rail's first regular freight contracts was that of the log traffic to Kronospan's site at Chirk (near Wrexham). Here 56113 heads east through Cardiff Central station with a loaded train from Baglan Bay on 15 July 2014.

The first 'log' flow for Colas was that from Carlisle to Chirk. In this view, 66849 *Wylam Dilly* passes south through Carlisle station shortly after departure from the yard. The date was 9 April 2015.

Felixstowe is Britain's busiest container port. The rail industry faces several challenges as it competes to handle onward movement of containers arriving here. The size of containers and rail gauging issues are compounded by the last few miles of line on the branch from Ipswich being non electrified. Ipswich itself is therefore a loco hub for diesel and electric loco stabling. On 8 July 2015 90044 is stabled at Ipswich awaiting its next duty.

On 5 October 2015, 90049 is awaiting its next call. It stands at Ipswich in its then new colours.

On the same day, 5 October 2015, 66414 is also on the Ipswich stabling point. It once sported the Stobart Rail house colours. By 2015 however it was resplendent in its new owner's colours.

On 8 July 2015, it's the turn of a pair of 70s to be found on Ipswich stabling point. Here, 70007 and 70019 take a break between Freightliner workings.

One of the most frequent freight flows in Scotland was the movement of imported coal from Hunterston to Longannet power station in Fife. Until the latter's closure in March 2016, coal was loaded via the former British Steel ore loading facility at Longannet in Ayrshire. On 31 March 2015, 66114 heads a loaded working eastbound through Greenfaulds in North Lanarkshire.

Colas also played its part in coal movement. Here 66848 heads south through Darlington on 13 June 2013. Its locally mined coal had been loaded at Wolsingham and was destined for Ratcliffe power station on this occasion.

Inevitably, Freightliner's Heavy Haul arm has suffered badly with the downturn in demand for rail movement of coal. Against the backdrop of its castle, 66508 heads south through Newcastle's Central station with loaded coal hoppers on 11 June 2013.

Coal is also moved by rail from the surface mine at Greenburn in Ayrshire. 66710 is seen on 1 March 2017 heading through Mexborough with empty hoppers from Ratcliffe to stable temporarily at Doncaster. The rake had earlier formed a loaded working from Greenburn to the Nottinghamshire power station.

All the main freight operators play a part in the ongoing maintenance and modification of the rail infrastructure. One large project involves the London Bridge upgrade. On 14 October 2015, 66148 (in the foreground) with 66144 are to be found within the Network Rail work site.

Engineering trains operate between various yards within the rail network. One regular working for Colas is from Westbury to Bescot. It is seen here at Nuneaton on 5 May 2016 with 66850 *David Maidment* working the train. It was also conveying 70805, 70806 and 70802 within its load.

This Westbury to Bescot working is seen again on 14 September 2015. This time 70804 is in charge of a rake of mixed wagons as it heads north through Oxford.

A much longer round trip working introduced in February 2017 sees a DRS move from Carlisle to Mountsorrel in Leicestershire and return. The empties travel southwards via the West Coast Main Line. The return loaded working is via Toton, York and Tyne. Here the return is captured approaching Chesterfield on 1 March 2017.

Freightliner is the largest intermodal railfreight operator in the UK, chiefly with traffic to/from the container ports of Felixstowe and Southampton. Here 66517 passes through Manchester Piccadilly, approaching its journey's end on 4 June 2015. It is working from Felixstowe to Trafford Park.

Another example, 66566, heads south through Northampton on the centre road on 15 May 2015. It is on a southbound working from Garston to Southampton.

These intermodal workings are often also used to offer locos a 'piggyback' between locations for positioning or maintenance reasons. On 21 February 2017, 66599 gives 66589 such a lift. It is seen here passing through Nuneaton working from Felixstowe to Ditton.

Freightliner operates a daily service between Bristol Railport and Felixstowe. Here, the eastbound working is seen passing through Acton Yard heading for the North London Line. It is hauled by 66568 on 19 June 2015.

The autumn leaf fall brings an annual challenge to the rail network. Rail Head Treatment Trains (RHTT) have run using pairs of locos for many years now. This often sees DRS Class 20/3s brought out of store for these workings. Here 20312 (with 20308) take a break at Sheffield on 23 October 2014. They are on a circuit to/ from Thrall's works at York.

In the 2015 season, a pair of DB 66s are seen arriving at Leicester on 19 October. 66101 and 66197 are about to reverse having just arrived from Peterborough.

Another pair of Class 66s, 66126 with 66098, pause at Bristol Temple Meads. They are on a Great Western RHTT diagram on 12 October 2013.

DB Cargo often provides pairs of Class 67s for the RHTT based from its Toton depot. This diagram covers the southern end of the Midland Main Line. The colourful pairing of 67018 *Keith Heller* and 67002 were to be found on this working passing through Bedford on 20 October 2016.

GBRf has a number of locos with one-off liveries among its fleet. Here 66718 is seen at Peterborough on 21 May 2014 with a WBB minerals working. It features GBRf's support for London Transport Museum. The loco also carries the name *Sir Peter Hendy CBE*, who was then the Commissioner of Transport for London.

GBRf's support for London Transport Museum is also featured in the livery applied to 66721. This loco depicts London's familiar Underground map designed by Harry Beck in the 1930s. 66721 is seen at the entrance to Hither Green yard on 23 September 2016. It also carries the *Harry Beck* nameplate.

66720 carries a livery that was judged the winner of a competition on a company-run family day out. This 'night and day' design was the brainchild of one of the children of a Whitemoor based company employee. It is seen here passing Leicester on 13 March 2017 on a Ferme Park to Bardon Hill working.

66727 was named *Maritime One* at Birch Coppice (near Tamworth) in September 2016. A corporate livery has also been applied, recognising the partnership between GBRf and Maritime Transport. Here the loco is heading through Nuneaton on 14 March 2017 working from Felixstowe to, appropriately, Birch Coppice.

All operators need to move empty wagons around the UK for various reasons and DRS are no exception. Here, 68003 *Astute* takes a rake of intermodal twin flats from Daventry to Motherwell. It is seen heading north through Nuneaton on 15 January 2015.

Veteran 47832 was used on a wagon move on 24 October 2013. The Northern Belle-liveried loco is seen here approaching the High Level at Tamworth with a new delivery of intermodal flats from W. H. Davis at Shirebrook to Daventry.

A Class 57 was used for another movement of flats on 7 February 2017. 57301 *Goliath* heads south through Nuneaton with a Crewe to Daventry working.

Chiltern Railways-liveried locomotives are seldom seen on freight-related workings. On 5 June 2015 68012 was called upon to move a solitary twin flat from Shirebrook to Derby. It is seen here drifting through Chesterfield.

DB Cargo has a dwindling number of Class 60s in its active loco pool. Oil tank trains to and from Humberside offer one of the more likely workings on which to find them. On 21 February 2017, 60007 *The Spirit of Tom Kendell* returns from Kingsbury to Lindsey Oil Refinery with a rake of empties through Tamworth.

A few days earlier and 60066 heads past the same location, Tamworth. This time the working is a loaded rake from Lindsey to Kingsbury on 1 February 2017. The loco carries the Drax's 'powering tomorrow' livery in connection with the biomass traffic.

DB Class 60s on the southern end of the Midland Main Line are rare since the company's 2015 loss of tank traffic between Lindsey and Colnbrook. 60039's appearance at Bedford on 27 August 2015 was unexpected. It is seen heading north with Heidelberg cement empties from St Pancras to Ketton (in Rutland).

South Wales also enjoys appearances from Class 60s on oil tank workings. Here, on 14 July 2015, 60092 heads west through Cardiff's Central station with a Theale to Margam working. The Murco terminal at Theale has since been acquired by Puma.

DB remains the chief operator of steel traffic in the UK. The majority of this traffic operates to and from the South Wales sites of Llanwern and Port Talbot with Margam as the rail hub. On 16 July 2015, 66113 approaches Cardiff Central with an eastbound working from Margam to Dollands Moor.

Several steel trains a week continue to operate between Corby and Margam. On 17 January 2017 66113 heads south through Leicester with the return empties from Corby to South Wales.

Another steel working heads west through Cardiff Central. This time it is 60020 working from East Usk Junction yard at Newport to Margam on 14 July 2015.

In this photo the steel is contained in cargo wagons and is destined for export. On 1 October 2015, 66188 heads through Barking with a working to Tilbury Docks from Tata's plant in Trostre (near Llanelli).

Freightliner has an important out-base at Earles Sidings on the Hope Valley Line in Derbyshire. From here Freightliner operates services for Hope Cement (part of the Breedon Group) to and from various UK destinations. On 5 October 2016 66604 works through Toton Yard with a loaded working to the depot at Walsall. DB's line of stored Class 60s is visible in the foreground.

Another important destination for Freightliner Heavy Haul is that of Theale (near Reading) where the rail-served facility has been upgraded. 66610 is seen on 19 January 2017 heading north through Leicester with the return empties from Theale to Earles Sidings.

These workings are more commonly handled by Class 66/6 locos with their lower gear ratio. Making a welcome change on 13 January 2017, 66519 works the same empties diagram. This time the train is captured northbound through Bedford.

Hope Cement at Earles Sidings also serves a recently opened depot at Dagenham in East London. On 23 December 2016 66616 approaches Bedford with a loaded working heading towards Dagenham.

Coal train movements in South Wales are in sharp decline as elsewhere in the UK. This was the only such working seen in a three-hour spell at Newport on 16 July 2015. 66025 heads west through the station with a rake of HTAs from East Usk Junction yard to Onllwyn Washery.

As already mentioned, Longannet power station has closed. Here is another example of the once frequent coal flow from Hunterston to that power station. On 12 June 2013 66158 heads east through Cumbernauld in North Lanarkshire.

Freightliner Class 66 66522 still carries its Shanks Group livery. It is seen here passing through Doncaster on 9 September 2013 with an unidentified northbound coal working.

Rugeley is another power station that has disappeared from the railway map. It received imported coal from Immingham Docks in the period leading up to its closure. On 16 February 2016, 66616 powers a rake of empties through Water Orton. They were being worked back from Rugeley to Barnetby sidings.

The Class 59s have spent most of their working lives concentrating on hauling stone trains from the West Country quarries. Acton in West London remains an important yard not least for splitting and joining of the so-called jumbo trains. 59205 and 59005 *Kenneth J Painter* are seen here on 19 June 2015.

An eastbound jumbo passes through Hayes and Harlington on 20 April 2016. 59002 *Alan J Day* is in charge of this Merehead to Acton working.

On 16 June 2015, 59004 *Paul A Hammond* arrives at Acton Yard on the same jumbo working. It will head eastwards later on its forward working with a portion of this rake.

These jumbo portions work to various locations in London and the south east. Here 59206 *John F Yeoman Rail Pioneer* passes through Gospel Oak on 22 September 2015 with a return portion from Harlow Mill. These wagons will be re-marshalled at Acton before heading further west.

Tonbridge is one of the main homes of GBRf's fleet of 73s. On 25 June 2016, 73109, 73136 *Tracy*, 73965, 73213 *Rhodalyn*, and 73962 *Dick Mabbutt* are all stabled awaiting their next turn of duty.

GBRf locos are also stabled at Eastleigh. Here on 3 October 2015, 66748 and 66744 share the sidings adjacent to the station along with other GB and Colas locos.

GBRf locos are also stabled at Hoo Junction near Higham in Kent. Here on 25 June 2016 were 66714 and 66752 *The Hoosier State* awaiting their departure on weekend engineering trains. The latter loco was the first numbered of a batch of 66s GBRf ordered from EMD's plant in Muncie, Indiana. Its name is a nickname for that state.

The small servicing depot at Peterborough sees a regular flows of Class 66s for examinations etc. On 20 January 2016, 66709 *Sorrento* is stabled outside with 66703 only partially visible inside the shed itself. 66709 carries a unique livery promoting Mediterranean Shipping Company (MSC).

The Class 86s soldier on in traffic with Freightliner despite having clocked up half a century in service. They can still be seen on the southern end of the WCML. Here 86614 leads 86613 through Bletchley on 21 April 2016. They are on an Ipswich to Trafford Park working.

On 8 June 2016, 86637 and 86614 give a lift to 90045. The trio are seen northbound through Stafford on a Felixstowe to Crewe liner. The electrics came on to the train at Ipswich.

The Class 90s have each notched up around thirty years' service. Freightliner's small pool also see regular use on freight traffic on WCML. Here 90048 heads south through Tamworth on 14 March 2017. The working is Trafford Park to Felixstowe and again the electric will be removed at Ipswich.

In this view it is the diesel's turn to hitch a ride. 90046 takes 66546 north through Rugeley Trent Valley on 18 July 2016. The working is from Felixstowe to Ditton.

In January 2017, DB Cargo branded two locos to promote the inaugural Yiwu (China) to London (Barking) intermodal service, for which it had charge here in the UK. Here 92015 carries its new branding as it is dragged south through Nuneaton by 66099 on 16 January in readiness for the resultant publicity on the first train's arrival.

The second loco with the Yiwu branding was 66136. It is seen here waiting for the road north from Leicester on 9 February 2016. On that day it was on a domestic modal duty from Burton on Trent to Felixstowe.

DB Cargo have also applied a promotional livery to 90024 to reflect its partnership with the Malcolm Group. It is partnered here with 90040 as it heads south through Tamworth on a Mossend to Daventry intermodal on 14 March 2017.

90024 previously carried Scotrail branding. It is seen here on 17 December 2015 in their colours. It was diagrammed to work van traffic in connection with Christmas extras between Warrington and Shieldmuir (Glasgow). It is seen here laying over against the wall at Carlisle between these workings.

A small amount of Royal Mail traffic continues to be handled by the rail industry. These workings are handled by a dedicated fleet of Class 325 units introduced in the mid-1990s. The main service is via the West Coast Main Line between Willesden (London), Warrington and Shieldmuir (Glasgow). Here 325011 is seen heading north through Bank Quay station, Warrington, on 10 July 2014.

These units can also be found on the East Coast Main Line. On 29 March 2015, 325004 is seen stabled in Tyne Yard between duties.

Despite a dramatic downturn in volume, cargo wagons can still be found on the UK network. Here 66116 heads a rake of these wagons through Tamworth on 27 January 2017. This working is from Dollands Moor to Ditton. It contains aluminium for Jaguar Land Rover's Merseyside works.

The Channel Tunnel continues to see a flow of bottled water in cargo wagons. On 12 December 2016, 90018 and 90037 perform on the Wembley to Daventry leg of this working. They are seen here heading through Milton Keynes Central.

Alongside its nuclear and intermodal diagrams, DRS locos are commonplace on Infrastructure workings. One regular weekday diagram sees a loco from their Gresty Bridge, Crewe depot pick up a rake of empties in Basford Hall yard and take to Mountsorrel for loading. On 21 March 2017, 68024 *Centaur* works the empties north through Leicester.

The loaded working returns to Crewe via Loughborough, Burton on Trent and Lichfield Trent Valley. On 19 October 2016, 68001 *Evolution* is captured heading north through Loughborough.

On 11 February 2014, this Crewe to Mountsorrel working was entrusted to a pair of Class 57s. On that day 57010 and 57008 are seen approaching Burton on Trent on their return working to Crewe.

Class 66s also appear on this diagram. On 7 March 2017, 66302 heads through Burton on Trent station with the loaded working returning to Crewe.

Not all intermodal traffic from Felixstowe travels via the outskirts of London. Peterborough sees an increasing number of workings from this busy container port. On 9 July 2016, 66025 heads for Wakefield Euro Terminal. It is seen passing Marholm (just north of Peterborough).

Further north on the ECML, 66743 heads south through Doncaster station on 3 February 2016 working from Selby to the Suffolk port. This traffic currently operates to and from Masborough (Rotherham) using the south curve and avoiding the station itself.

DP World London Gateway (near Thurrock in Essex) is becoming increasingly important in UK container movement by rail. One regular service sees traffic to and from Trafford Park (Manchester). On 22 September 2015 66007 heads the Manchester-bound working through Upper Holloway.

On 4 May 2016 the southbound working snakes its way between Oxford Road and Piccadilly stations in Manchester. 66077 *Benjamin Gimbert GC* is at the helm. It is one of only a handful of DB 66s to carry a name.

Peak Forest in Derbyshire sees a number of regular rail traffic flows for the construction industry. On 22 March 2015 (a Sunday), 60092 heads west through Edale in the Hope Valley with a rake of empties returning to Peak Forest from Attercliffe (Sheffield).

On 9 July 2014 60074 *Teenage Spirit* approaches Manchester Victoria. It has just left the Cemex site at Hope Street, Salford, on its return journey to Peak Forest. The loco received its name and a distinctive blue livery as part of a charity event linked to the Teenage Cancer Trust.

Redundant HTA coal hoppers are now finding use on the Peak Forest construction traffic. On 11 January 2017, 66025 leaves the Marston Vale branch and joins the Midland Main Line at Bedford with return empties from Cemex's depot at Bletchley.

This rake of loaded HTAs is seen through Doncaster on 2 February 2017. DB repainted 66152 *Derek Holmes Railway Operator* is seen working from Peak Forest to Potter Group at Selby.

Jaguar Land Rover (JLR) use rail to move cars for export. On 27 January 2017, 66103 pauses at Nuneaton for a crew change on one of the regular flows. This working is from JLR's plant at Halewood on Merseyside to Southampton Eastern Docks. The train is routed away from the WCML at this point to head through Coventry and Didcot to its destination.

Cars are also transported using double-deck covered carriers (WIAs). 66125 is seen shunting some of these wagons at Didcot Parkway on 18 April 2015.

The Dagenham to Garston car flow is a recent gain by GBRf. It can produce a Class 66 or Class 92 for haulage. On 14 March 2017, the loaded working is seen through Tamworth heading north behind 66751 *Inspiration Delivered – Hitachi Rail Europe*.

Electric loco power was provided on 26 January 2016. On that day, 92033 is seen passing the same location, Tamworth, with the Garston-bound working.

There is still variety in the tank trains found on the network today, at least in terms of the contents. GBRf operate the traffic to and from Harwich to North Walsham on the branch line from Norwich to Cromer and Sheringham. Here 66704 *Colchester Power Signalbox* hauls the loaded gas condensate tanks through Ipswich on 8 July 2015.

Colas now handles the flow from Lindsey (Humberside) to Colnbrook in West London. From the terminal here the aviation fuel is piped to Heathrow Airport. Following the discharge of its train 60052 works back north with the empties on 15 April 2016. It is seen here approaching Wellingborough.

Colas also handles the bitumen workings from Lindsey to Preston. On 27 February 2015, 60076 returns the discharged tanks to Humberside. The Barnetby semaphores are no more.

Today, there are only a few fuel trains that serve the rail sector itself. One such working is the weekly flow from Lindsey to Neville Hill depot (Leeds). On 23 July 2014, 66012 approaches Leeds City station heading for the depot with the loaded working.

The sand train from Middleton Towers (near King's Lynn) to Warrington Arpley/Ellesmere Port is often referred to as the 'mobile desert' or 'mobile beach'. Here 66014 demonstrates why. It is seen passing Marholm (north of Peterborough) on 4 July 2015 bound for Warrington Arpley.

GBRf have signed an extended contract for movements for WBB Minerals out of Middleton Towers. 66711 *Sence* heads through Doncaster on 2 February 2017 with a working from Middleton Towers to Monk Bretton. The loco name relates to the geographic environs around Bardon Hill in Leicestershire.

These wagon moves are often used as a means of light engines getting a lift between GBRf's stabling points at Peterborough and Doncaster. On 12 July 2014, 66712 *Peterborough Power Box* heads from Doncaster to Peterborough through Marholm. It is giving a lift to 66732 *GBRf The First Decade 1999–2009 John Smith – MD*, 66718 *Sir Peter Hendy CBE*, and 66748.

On 25 April 2015, 66735 is also seen heading past Marholm. It is working from Peterborough to Doncaster with 66713 *Forest City*, 66765 and 66748 for company.

Household waste is moved by rail by several freight operators. DB cargo 66058 *Derek Clark* sits alongside West Hampstead Thameslink station on 22 September 2015. It has just run rounds its wagons on arrival from Cricklewood and is waiting to head to the landfill site at Calvert in Buckinghamshire.

North of the border the contract to handle some of Edinburgh's waste by rail has just ended. For many years Class 67s had been the mainstay on these workings. On 30 March 2015, 67025 *Western Star* is pictured at Oxwellmains landfill site near Dunbar. It had arrived from the waste transfer station at Powderhall.

Manchester is another city committed to moving waste by rail. 66508 is seen near Manchester Victoria on 9 July 2014 heading for Dean Lane on the east side of the city.

66553 heads another Freightliner working from the Manchester area through Sheffield on 2 July 2013. Its destination is the landfill site at Roxby near Scunthorpe.

Freightliner Heavy Haul has seen a dramatic downturn in volumes of coal being moved in the UK. In busier times, 66595 hauls a westbound train through Worksop on 21 March 2014.

Doncaster station has also witnessed a dramatic downturn in the number of coal trains passing through. On 8 January 2014, 66585 *The Drax Flyer* heads south towards Decoy yard.

The downturn has also affected the Freightliner western out-base at Stoke Gifford. On Sunday 7 July 2013, 70013 is one of that yard's weekend occupants.

Several Class 70s are currently out of use at Leeds's Midland Road depot. On 27 January 2017, 70009 leads a row of classmates stabled adjacent to the running lines.

Flows of scrap metal tend to be short term or irregular contracts. EMR at Kingsbury is served by 66055 on 27 January 2015. It is seen passing through Water Orton with the empties for Cardiff Tidal on their way for loading.

Back in 2014, Freightliner were responsible for a scrap flow from Crewe to Aldwarke (near Rotherham). Eyebrows were raised on 23 May that year when Colas's 70809 was hired in to work this service. It is seen heading south through Chesterfield with the return empties.

On 19 June 2015, 56312 is seen approaching Acton. This Devon & Cornwall Railways machine was working the return empty spoil wagons from Calvert to Willesden. The loco's lengthy name is *Jeremiah Dixon – Son of County Durham Surveyor of the Mason – Dixon Line USA*.

On 27 January 2014, the GBRf pair of 73212 *Fiona* and 73207 were also to be found on a spoil diagram. They are seen here about to pass under the bridge at Willesden, approaching journey's end at the Euro Terminal there.

Eastleigh remains a magnet for freight enthusiasts in the south of England. On Sunday morning 4 October 2015, 70803 heads a weekend engineers train out of the yard.

On 30 August 2013, 66035 heads north towards Eastleigh station with a rake of empty cartics from Southampton's Eastern Docks.

One of the longer distance flows to Eastleigh emanates from Scunthorpe delivering long welded rail. Haulage is usually a DB Cargo Class 66. On 19 July 2016, 66037 is in charge as the working heads through Chesterfield.

As the crow flies the working from Hoo Junction to Eastleigh covers a much shorter distance. It does however take a circuitous route from Kent to Hampshire – via the London suburbs. On 30 June 2016, 66719 *Metro-Land* takes a short rake through Clapham Junction.

East Sussex boasts few freight workings. GBRf does, however, have a contract to move loaded gypsum traffic from the mine at Mountfield near Robertsbridge. On 25 June 2016, 66706 *Nene Valley* heads north through Tonbridge with a working destined for Southampton Docks.

At almost the other end of England, DB's 66128 heads through Doncaster working gypsum wagons from the yards there to Gascoigne Wood. The date is 7 January 2015.

Ironbridge power station's conversion to 100 per cent biomass fuel was shortlived. It ceased production towards the end of 2015. On 27 August 2014, 66702 *Blue Lightning* heads north through Stafford with empty biomass wagons from the power station. They were returning to Liverpool Docks.

The biomass flow from Immingham to Drax power station continues. On 2 February 2017, 66076 heads a loaded rake west through Barnetby past the now defunct East signal box.

Hope Construction's cement works in Derbyshire provides Freightliner with a number of daily workings to various distribution depots within the Breedon Group. Earles sidings in the Hope Valley is the destination of 66605. It is seen here heading north through Chesterfield on 17 July 2014. This empty working had commenced its journey from Theale (near Reading).

The same empties working is seen again on 11 September 2015. This time the loco in charge was 66623 *Bill Bolsover*. It once sported full Bardon Aggregates livery denoting Freightliner's previous links with that company's distributions.

Hope Construction also moves much of its aggregate from Dowlow limestone quarry near Buxton by rail. DB operate a regular flow to their rail served depot in Walsall. On 16 February 2016, 66105 is seen working the return empties through Water Orton.

The same working is seen again on 31 January 2017. By then, new box wagons were in use on the service. It is captured here approaching Tamworth with 66003 in charge.

DRS has extended its range of services beyond that of the nuclear flask traffic. It operates a number of intermodal services. Here, 66428 approaches Carlisle while working from Daventry to Coatbridge on 9 April 2015. This loco was involved in a collision in Ayrshire later that year and only returned to traffic in June 2017.

DRS also introduced a number of feeder services within Scotland. On 5 April 2015, 66421 heads north through Perth with a working from Grangemouth to Aberdeen.

The Highland line sees a daily feeder service from Mossend to Inverness. On 2 April 2015, 66427 passes through Pitlochry with the southbound return service.

DRS also operate a regular weekday service between Daventry and Purfleet Deep Water Wharf. On 8 October 2015, 66305 heads through Barking while working the eastbound service.

Freight operators have found lucrative business moving a wide variety of empty stock for other rail companies. One such contract involved moving new London Underground (LUL) units between Derby, Old Dalby (test track) and West Ruislip onto LUL itself. On 19 March 2014, 20096 and 20107 are seen at Derby on one such move.

Freightliner have a contract for moving new Class 387 units between Derby and Bletchley prior to mileage accumulation runs from the latter depot. On 13 October 2016, 66953 heads south through Market Harborough dragging C2C unit 387303 to Bletchley.

GBRf have an ongoing contract to move 'Networker' units between SouthEastern's Slade Green (Dartford) base and Wabtec's works at Doncaster. 66701 heads through Marholm (north of Peterborough) on 9 July 2016, taking 465923 to the Yorkshire workshops.

The Rail Operations Group (ROG) regularly secures these 'unit drag' contracts using their small fleet of heritage locos. One ongoing contract involves the moves of Class 375 units between their home depot of Ramsgate and Litchurch Lane at Derby. On 18 December 2016, and in fading light, 37800 drags 375907 northwards through Bedford.

One of the remaining regular freight flows through the Channel Tunnel sees steel move between Ebange (in France) and Scunthorpe. The UK leg of this working from Dollands Moor is seen north of Sandy on 29 January 2017. Loco 66185 *DP World London Gateway* is at the head of the empty twin flats.

This empty steel working is occasionally used to move ECR Class 66s between the Channel Tunnel and Scunthorpe – for onward movement from there back south to Toton. On 7 January 2017, 66145 gives a lift to 66052 and 66022. It is seen here heading north through Hitchin in a rainstorm.

DB Cargo also handles steel movements to and from the steel terminal at Wolverhampton. On 19 January 2017, 66206 heads a return rake of empties from the terminal to Immingham.

These workings reach Wolverhampton via Bescot Yard. On 18 March 2016, 66172 approaches Tame Bridge Parkway, at the southern end of the yard, with a return rake of empties for Masborough (Rotherham).

In 2014 Colas purchased ten Class 60s from DB Cargo (then DB Schenker). On 28 January 2017, one of its purchases is back on old territory. It stands on DB's Toton depot alongside former stablemate 60091.

Two more of Colas's Class 60s were to be seen on Tyne Yard on 29 March 2016. 60002 and 60087 are top'n'tail there with a Railvac.

The work for these Colas Class 60s includes tank traffic out of Immingham. For this purpose they now stable in Barnetby yard. On 2 February 2017, 60026 and 60047 are seen there (viewed here through the windows of a Class 185 unit).

Another top'n'tail Class 60 pairing is seen accompanying a Railvac on 2 July 2016. 60096, with 60076 on the rear, head south through Bedford working from Toton to Hendon.

Freightliner operate the Willesden to Cliffe Hill Stud Farm ballast circuit. This takes a circuitous route to the Leicestershire quarry via the West Midlands. On 13 December 2016 the outbound working is seen heading through Rugby behind 66418 *Patriot In Memory of Fallen Railway Employees.*

On 29 September 2016, the Whitemoor to Parkeston Quay engineers working produces a pair of Freightliner 66s. 66510 leads 66537 through Ipswich with a mixed rake of wagons.

Freightliner's 66547 is in charge of the High Output Ballast Cleaner (HOBC) on 19 October 2016. It is seen heading south through Leicester working from Stapleford to Luton.

The length, and weight, of the HOBC is contrasted by this ballast working. On 1 September 2014, 66524 is seen with a rake of just seven loaded IOA wagons heading through Loughborough. It is on a return working from Mountsorrel to Toton.

Not only do freight customers switch operators but the operators themselves often switch between their traction options. The UK tank traffic is no exception. The Humber to Kingsbury tanks, once a Freightliner contract, is currently in the hands of DB Cargo. 60s used to be the cornerstone of these workings but Class 66s also take their turn. On 7 January 2015 the loaded working from Humber Oil Refinery passes Barnetby behind 66148.

Puma Energy acquired the terminal at Bedworth from Murco in March 2015. The 'new customer' now uses GBRf to take deliveries from Immingham. On 9 February 2017, 66723 *Chinook* is in charge of the return working. It is seen at Nuneaton having just left the Warwickshire terminal.

Colas has been successful in securing additional tank traffic at the expense of DB Cargo. The latter had control of the Lindsey to Colnbrook flow back in 2014. On 5 September that year, 66068 heads north through Bedford with the return empties.

The tank traffic from Lindsey to Rectory Junction (near Nottingham) has also switched from DB Cargo to Colas operation. On 15 March 2015, 60021 reaches Newark Northgate station with the return empties for Lindsey.

GBRf's sole Class 59 can often be found on workings that involve a 'circle' from Bardon Hill. This circuit includes a flow from Tinsley (near Sheffield) to Coton Hill (near Shrewsbury). On 19 January 2017, 59003 *Yeoman Highlander* is seen passing through Tamworth.

North of the border GBRF are responsible for one of the most remote freight flows in the UK. The Alcan traffic operates from North Blyth (in Northumberland) to Fort William via the West Highland line (WHL). On 4 February 2014, 66737 *Lesia* is seen in more urban surroundings as it passes through Springburn in the Glasgow suburbs heading for the WHL.

The iron ore workings on Humberside were always popular among Class 60 enthusiasts. For many years of DB operation they were the traction mainstay. On 15 January 2013, 60011 heads through Barnetby working the return empties from Santon (Scunthorpe) to Immingham.

Colas's entry into the freight sector saw a number of heritage machines have their working lives extended. The steel flow from Boston Docks to Washwood Heath saw the use of both Class 47 and 56 traction. On 26 January 2016, 56087 heads north through Tamworth with a rake of ten curtain siders destined for the Lincolnshire port.

The yards at Toton and Bescot continue to be two of the main Midlands hubs for infrastructure engineering traffic. On 3 November 2016 the pairing of 90010 and 90037 *Spirit of Dagenham* are unusual traction for a return working of brightly coloured MXA's (nicknamed 'lobsters') from Wembley to Bescot. They are seen approaching Milton Keynes Central.

One of the long-standing regular weekday flows for DB is the working between these two Midlands yards. On 1 February 2017, traction comes in the form of 66027. It is seen passing Tamworth on the lunchtime Toton-bound working.

Toton sees the making up of engineering trains in readiness for weekend duties wherever they are required in the area. On 28 January 2017, a Saturday, 66207, 66130, 66031, and 66011 are all ready for their departures.

Destinations can be just about anywhere from main line to branch or freight-only lines. On 19 February 2017, a Sunday, 66128 is returning from one such duty on the Marston Vale line. It is seen heading north through Bedford on the return working from Forders (Stewartby) to Toton.

Weekend engineering duties often mean repositioning of locos after completion of their normal weekday responsibilities. This can lead to loco convoys in multiple. On 26 May 2012, one such move saw no fewer than seven DB Class 66 locos pass eastwards through Cardiff Central. They were heading from Margam to Westbury. For the record the locos are (from nearest) 66080, 66131, 66105, 66050, 66057, 66213, and 66040.

GBRf moves between their bases on or near the ECML have already been mentioned. On Sunday 9 March 2014, 66729 *Derby County*, 66721, 66732, 66704, and 66702 are heading from Peterborough to Doncaster in readiness for the new working week. They are seen passing Marholm.

Freightliner light engine moves can often be seen in the vicinity of Crewe station. On 30 October 2014, 86638, 86613, 90046, and 70017 are in the platform next to the Shrewsbury bay. They are reversing in a move that will take them from one side of the WCML to the other.

DB Cargo also have a regular need to move locos between their bases at Crewe and Willesden/Wembley. On 28 February 2017, a southbound move through Nuneaton sees 90029 lead 92016 and 92011 *Handel*.

Despite diesel power outnumbering the electric fleet many times over, there are still many workings for these electrics on the WCML. At the beginning of 2017, Freightliner have used pairs of Class 90s on some Anglo-Scottish workings between Daventry and Coatbridge. On 19 January 2017, 90047 is paired with 90048 as it heads through Nuneaton on a northbound working.

DB Cargo also entrusts pairs of Class 90s on its Daventry to Mossend services. On 24 January 2017, 90028 leads 90035 on a Daventry-bound service passing Nuneaton.

Class 92 traction use on the WCML is now infrequent. GBRf used 92032 *IMechE Railway Division* on 12 March 2015 to work between Daventry, Wembley and Dollands Moor. It is seen passing through Milton Keynes Central.

On 30 October 2014, 92044 *Couperin* is seen further north. It is captured through Sandbach while on an intermodal working to Trafford Park.

DRS handle a regular engineers traffic flow between Crewe, Dollands Moor and Toton on an 'as required' basis. On 5 June 2014, 66431 takes charge of this working as it heads through Nuneaton on the Bescot to Toton leg. Its load on this occasion is three JNA wagons.

Just a few weeks earlier on 10 May that year, Network Rail yellow-liveried 57312 made a welcome change on the same working. It is again seen through Water Orton, this time with a slightly longer rake. The loco carried the name *Peter Henderson* at the time of this photo.

DRS also handle engineering traffic on the ECML. In particular, there are regular workings between York and Doncaster. On 26 January 2017, the northbound return is in the charge of 68021 *Tireless* as it passes through Doncaster station.

The Chiltern-liveried examples of the Class 68 fleet are occasionally seen on these ballast duties. On 19 May 2016, 68013 heads north through Leicester on the inbound empties on the day's Crewe to Mountsorrel.

The use of freight traction on Network Rail test trains continues. These workings have been handled in recent years by a wide variety of motive power from several companies. DRS Class 68s found use on a Derby to Old Oak Common working on 16 September 2016. 68005 *Defiant* and 68021 are seen reversing in Derby station before taking the Burton line to head to west London.

Freightliner Class 90s are also to be found on stock moves in conjunction with the Scotrail sleeper services. On 9 November 2016, 90043 can be seen in Wembley Yard shunting the empty stock of one of that morning's Euston arrivals. This view was taken from passing the yard on a Class 350 unit.

Despite all the latest technology and up-to-date information, it can still be fun when something just turns up. A last minute working through Tamworth on 1 February 2017 was one such example. 66112 appeared with two Mark 1 coaches – a brake composite and a generator van – heading from Crewe to Nemesis Rail at Burton on Trent.

There are other publications that concentrate on so-called freight traction working passenger trains. Therefore, just one example is included here. 37419 *Carl Haviland 1954 – 2012* waits at Great Yarmouth on 16 June 2016. It will lead the short set on the return service to Norwich.